THE BIG REVEAL

Loving Your LGBTQ+ Child While Strengthening Your Faith

Foreword by Justin Lee

Debbie Causey

WESTBOW PRESS®
A DIVISION OF THOMAS NELSON
& ZONDERVAN

Copyright © 2022 Debbie Causey.

All rights reserved. No part of this book may be used or reproduced by any means, graphic, electronic, or mechanical, including photocopying, recording, taping or by any information storage retrieval system without the written permission of the author except in the case of brief quotations embodied in critical articles and reviews.

This book is a work of non-fiction. Unless otherwise noted, the author and the publisher make no explicit guarantees as to the accuracy of the information contained in this book and in some cases, names of people and places have been altered to protect their privacy.

WestBow Press books may be ordered through booksellers or by contacting:

WestBow Press
A Division of Thomas Nelson & Zondervan
1663 Liberty Drive
Bloomington, IN 47403
www.westbowpress.com
844-714-3454

Because of the dynamic nature of the Internet, any web addresses or links contained in this book may have changed since publication and may no longer be valid. The views expressed in this work are solely those of the author and do not necessarily reflect the views of the publisher, and the publisher hereby disclaims any responsibility for them.

Any people depicted in stock imagery provided by Getty Images are models, and such images are being used for illustrative purposes only. Certain stock imagery © Getty Images.

Scripture quotations taken from The Holy Bible, New International Version® NIV® Copyright © 1973 1978 1984 2011 by Biblica, Inc. TM. Used by permission. All rights reserved worldwide.

Interior Image Credit: Go Pride Chicago

ISBN: 978-1-6642-6241-6 (sc)
ISBN: 978-1-6642-6240-9 (e)

Print information available on the last page.

WestBow Press rev. date: 04/30/2022

Contents

Foreword vii

Chapter 1   The Reveal 1
Chapter 2   Context 11
Chapter 3   Words of Wisdom 17
Chapter 4   Write It All Down 25
Chapter 5   Empathy Grows 33
Chapter 6   The Suicide Rate is Real 41
Chapter 7   This Can Shake Their Faith 47
Chapter 8   You Don't Have to Choose 59
Chapter 9   Keep It Safe 63
Chapter 10 You Will Be Okay 71

Conclusion: The Ultimate Reveal 79
About the Author 83

Foreword

I wish this book could have existed when I was a teenager. It would have meant a lot to my parents as they were struggling with some tough questions, and it might have helped me to better understand what they were going through.

I grew up in a deeply devout Christian family, much like the one Debbie describes in this book. None of us imagined we would ever have to deal with anything LGBTQ-related. Eventually, though, I had to confess to my parents that I had been wrestling for years with questions about my sexuality and that I had begun to suspect that I was gay.

They were shocked. And none of us knew quite what to do.

My parents knew they loved me, and they knew they wanted to guide me in the way of Jesus. But right from the beginning, they had a lot of questions—most of which I didn't learn about until years later:

Why had this happened?

Was it their fault?

How could they manage their feelings of grief and loss without heaping guilt on me for not turning out like they expected?

What should they do if I ultimately made choices they didn't approve of?

Who could they turn to for support in a church community where these discussions still felt so taboo?

My parents prayed fervently, studied the Scriptures, talked to our pastor, and read every book they could find, but they kept coming up with more questions than answers. And while they trusted God to guide us through what seemed like uncharted territory, I now know that they struggled with a lot of loneliness and self-doubt through it all.

Debbie Causey knows what that struggle is like, because she's lived it, too.

Debbie is a Christian mom who loves God and loves her kids, and she isn't willing to compromise on either. Like my parents, she found herself on a journey she never expected to be on, sparked by a revelation about her own child she never expected to hear.

But while it might not have been what she planned, God has used that journey to teach Debbie powerful lessons—and ultimately, to make a difference in the lives of so many other parents who are on the same road. Debbie's wisdom, experience, and grace have earned her respect in the eyes of those who know her, and I'm so excited she's agreed to write this book to share what she's learned with a wider audience.

All those years ago, without the benefit of a resource like Debbie's, my parents and I really wrestled with big questions about what God wanted us to do. We didn't always agree. Sometimes we clashed. Sometimes it seemed like we might never see eye to eye again.

But in the end, God faithfully brought us through the storm. God changed my heart on some things, and God changed my parents' hearts on some things. We kept our faith in Christ and love for each other intact, and today, I've been in public ministry for 25 years, helping other families navigate these challenging waters.

And make no mistake, these waters are challenging, especially now. Our culture is polarized, and many Christians and LGBTQ people have strongly negative views of each other. Sadly, I know too many people who think all Christians are simply hateful, bigoted, and judgmental.

But in these pages, you'll see a Christian mom who defies that stereotype. Her heart is here on every page—a heart overflowing with the love of God.

The Big Reveal is filled with so many wonderful insights and practical bits of wisdom for navigating this journey well. Debbie doesn't settle for easy answers or pretend to know everything in God's mind. Instead, she approaches these questions with Christian humility, vulnerability, faith, and love.

There are many challenging questions for us as Christians when we explore what God has to say to us about sexuality and gender. But if we all follow Debbie's example and lead with the kind of grace she demonstrates, I am certain we will see God use those challenges to make us better people and strengthen our faith and our families.

Justin Lee
Author
Torn: Rescuing the Gospel from the Gays-vs.-Christians Debate

Chapter One

The Reveal

When our oldest, Alston, and his wife, McKenzie, were a few months away from welcoming their first child—our first grandchild—into the family, we gathered together for a special gender reveal celebration. Cupcakes were prepared with icing the color of the gender inside waiting to be known. We each bit into our cupcake and it was…blue. Immediately, it all felt real. I went from thinking about Alston and McKenzie's baby to thinking about *my grandson*. With the reveal of this one, simple, biological fact, XX or XY, I gained joyous insight into who this new life would be.

The idea for this kind of celebration occurred well after my four children were born, but I will never forget the moment I learned our youngest, Noah, was a boy.

Just like we did with his three older siblings, we spent years learning everything we could about our youngest child. From day one, Noah was the sweetest, cuddliest, easiest baby. He slept 12 hours a night by 10 weeks. He took glorious, two to three hour naps. Even after he outgrew his naps, he would often proclaim, "I'm tired" and put himself to bed before 8 o'clock.

Noah was known for his ability to chill. Even when he

was in a stroller, he would lay back with his barefoot feet propped up on the bar. Shoes were not for him. They were kicked off any time I would put them on. He was content no matter what situation you put him in. He was along for the ride, sitting back and enjoying every minute of it.

On long car rides we rarely heard a peep from Noah. He enjoyed listening to everyone else share about their experiences from our time together or their latest stories with their friends. In fact, we rarely heard words from Noah in general. He was and is a quiet introvert who loves others to be the center of attention.

Maybe Noah's go-with-the-flow personality came with being the youngest. Maybe it was just who God made him to be. Probably, it was a little of both. Not only did Noah not make waves, he didn't like others to make waves either. Morality was Noah's middle name. He loved for others to do the right thing, say the right thing, and act the right way. He would get very frustrated when others used inappropriate language, lied, or broke the moral code he thought we should all live by. I could probably count on one hand the number of times he needed discipline. I remember my husband, Al, and I actually worrying he might be *too* good and that he would be made fun of for his rule-following tendencies.

Noah came to know Jesus at a young age and almost immediately got involved in our church. Because we attend a large church, Noah was able to find his place on stage, serving as a host or Bible storyteller for hundreds of preschoolers. He even served smaller groups of kids as their main leader week after week. He always strived to be good, to *do* good.

Which is partly why I was so unprepared for what Noah revealed to me when he was 17 years old.

It was 10 o'clock at night, and I was sitting in my favorite oversized chair. I had just finished listening to a two-hour saga from my 21-year-old daughter. I was already emotionally spent when Noah came down the stairs, plopped himself next to me, put his head on my chest, and began to cry uncontrollably. Startled does not begin to describe how I felt at that moment. He had never cried like this. I immediately held him close and asked him what was wrong. And what he revealed changed my world forever.

"Mom, I'm gay."

Thoughts flooded my mind. Panic coursed through my body. Nausea filled my stomach. *Was he kidding? Was this some kind of practical joke?* My family loves to joke around. But, no, he was sobbing. This couldn't be a joke. It was time for me to respond. *What was I supposed to say? Should I say what I wanted to say? Should I say what I believe? Should I just say nothing?* All I could think was, *Oh please, Lord, NO!*

Noah had always been a little different than the rest of my kids. He liked to play with his sister's Polly Pockets. He always played with the neighborhood girls and had no interest in the sports the boys played. In fact, he never liked sports at all but indulged our family (with two older brothers and a tomboy big sister) when we wanted to play a game of football or kickball as a family. Instead, Noah's true passion was theater. He did his first dramatic sketch for our church at the age of seven. He was such a natural that he was labeled "the one who would be famous one day."

Over the years, some of Noah's behavior was a little alarming for conservative parents like us, but we shrugged it off easily enough.

When Noah was nine, he went to play at his best friend Abby's house, hid in her closet, and tried on her cheerleading uniform. When Abby's mom filled me in on what happened, I remember thinking that was a little strange, but chalked it up to kids being silly sometimes.

A couple of years later, Noah spent the day with my mom. When he returned with mascara on, my mom said he was curious what it was like to wear makeup, so she'd let him play around with hers on the drive home. We immediately took him to the bathroom to clean it off. I remember how incredibly uncomfortable I was seeing my son's beautiful, extremely long eyelashes accentuated.

But one of the strangest moments came when Noah was a freshman in high school. Curious as to why we hadn't heard about any girls he was interested in, we asked him if he had a girlfriend or a crush. He quickly answered, "Nah, girls are a hassle."

What 15-year-old boy thinks girls are too much of a hassle to date or even have a crush on? We had two older boys, and by 15, girls seemed to occupy no less than 95% of their thoughts. While that alarmed us, once again we denied it was anything other than a funny thing to say, because he was kind of right—girls *can* be a hassle.

Still, while we saw signs over the years that Noah was unique, I was in no way prepared for him to come out to me in a sobbing heap that spring night.

Sitting in stunned silence with Noah shaking in the chair beside me, I somehow mustered up the words to say, "I couldn't love you any more than I do now, Noah, and I would never want to change you."

I wouldn't? What was I saying? If I had a magic wand in that moment, without hesitation I would have changed him. If I had a pill to make him straight, I would have asked him to take it. The only explanation for my ability to speak those words is what I believe to be the Holy Spirit. God gave me the strength and wisdom to know my initial reaction could damage my child—and our relationship—for a lifetime.

Then Noah said the words that have haunted me ever since: "Why did God make me this way?"

Between sobs he explained, "I have tried to change for the past four years, and it just isn't working. I don't want to be this way. Why would God make me this way?"

I had no words. I prayed for the Holy Spirit to give me more. All that came to mind was, "Noah, I don't know why God would allow you to be this way, but one thing I know for sure is that he loves you this way."

We held each other for another hour and a half as Noah continued to reveal all kinds of new (to me) insights: he had never been attracted to a girl; he didn't want to be alone for the rest of his life; he had a crush on guy in his theater troupe; and he had known he was gay since he was 13.

That last one made my whole body ache. Four years. My son had carried this *alone, in silence*, for four years.

It was so much to take in. I was bursting with questions: "Do other people know?", "Have you acted on these feelings?", "Do you think it's a sin to have a relationship with another guy?", "What kind of pornography have you looked at?"

The Holy Spirit continued to nudge me. "Noah, I know you didn't choose this. Who would choose this? And I don't want to change you or fix you. I love you and accept you right now as you are."

I assured Noah he wouldn't have to struggle alone any longer and that we would figure this out together. I told him I was sorry our home environment made him feel unsafe to tell us sooner and promised we would work hard to make it a safer place for him to confide in us.

Noah finally gathered himself together and went to bed, leaving me alone in my chair, shocked and bewildered. I was still staring off down the dark hallway, feeling completely numb, when Al came in the door a few minutes later. I must have looked whiter than a sheet because he immediately asked what was wrong. I told him the news and instantly recognized my own white-faced astonishment reflected in his face.

Yet again the Holy Spirit nudged me, and I told my husband, "You have to go upstairs and lay in bed with Noah. Hold him tight and tell him that you love him." I can't explain how, but I knew it was what Noah needed in that moment. He knew his dad was coming home and was terrified to tell him—not because my gentle, loving husband would flip out, but because Noah didn't want his dad to look at him differently. Noah didn't want his dad to be disgusted by him.

Al could hardly move, but willingly did what I pled with him to do. Noah was still crying and Al joined him. They held each other for a while, Al crying and reassuring Noah that he loved him.

Around midnight, Al came down and joined me in shell-shocked silence. I opened my computer to draft a message to my friend Amy. Despite being happily married to a man and having three kids of their own, she had confided in me that she was gay. I knew Amy was the only person who could help me. I needed to hear from someone who knew about this from personal experience.

12:16 AM April 23, 2014

Amy,

Please keep this confidential, but Al and I really need to talk to you right now. I am calling in sick tomorrow, but would like to see if you could come by at some point tomorrow to talk with Al and I. I don't think I am going to be able to do the talk on Thursday to the staff either and may need you to do that, but can explain more tomorrow. Is there any chance you could come over tomorrow at some point confidentially? Maybe at 10:00 or after your appt. at 3:00? I am in a really bad spot, and we need some wisdom. There is no one else to reach out to. I need my friend. Please text me to let me know if you can come and don't tell anyone where you are going please if you can come.

I am not sure if I am going to be able to sleep tonight, so I may look awful when you come over. Just a heads up.

Thank you,

Debbie

It was hard to put words to the emotions we were experiencing. There were so many at once. Terrified. Devastated. Worried. Protective. Guilty. Dumbfounded. Mystified. Disappointed. Depressed. So.very.*alone*.

The thoughts continued to swarm in our minds until 3 a.m. when we finally went to bed. Al and I both called in sick the next day, and a few days later we actually became physically sick from the stress we'd been experiencing.

Amy came over first thing in the morning. When she walked through the door, I burst into tears. We sat in our family room and filled her in on what had unfolded the previous night. When there were no more details left to share, we sat together—all of us emotionally depleted—not knowing what to say or do.

Slowly, Amy began to speak. "Everything is going to be okay. I know this feels like an overwhelming situation, but it will get easier with time. You both handled it so well, and

Noah is going to be better for it. So many parents do not, and their kids suffer greatly." She provided much-needed comfort and wisdom as we navigated what to do and say next. She gave us articles and suggested books that could help us begin to navigate what we were experiencing. And in that moment, we didn't feel so alone. Amy understood what we (Noah included) were going through.

We could not make sense of much that day or even that week, but one thing Al and I decided a couple of days after The Reveal was to never do or say anything that would make Noah feel alone. He had already experienced that desperation for four years. We now saw it as our job to do everything possible to make sure he never again felt an ounce of separation from our love.

For days, Noah's words—"Mom, I'm gay."—echoed in my mind. *My son is gay. I can't believe my son is gay. Is this a dream? Is this a nightmare?* It seemed my mind would never stop racing. I wondered if I would ever be able to go back to work and think about anything else.

I had so many questions I wanted to ask him. But Noah had been strategic in his timing, revealing this piece of himself to us just before the opening week of his spring play. Anyone who knows theater knows opening week means rehearsals and performances until 10 or 11 every night. We had no access to our son. For better or worse, we had no way of asking Noah what we thought we needed to know. So the questions started stacking up. I began making a mental (and at times physical) list of all the things I would ask him the second I had the chance.

But as my questions and thoughts stacked up, I began to realize many didn't make sense. So many of them came from my previously held beliefs about homosexuality. But my category for being gay had been shattered in an instant.

Before Noah's big reveal, I thought most gay people had

an agenda, a perpetual picket sign in their hand. I thought a gay person's sole objective was to flaunt their sexuality before me. I thought gay people had been broken somewhere along the way, had turned to some sexual perversion, and were giving in to sin.

But Noah didn't fit this category. He wasn't broken. He hadn't been perverted. He wasn't confused. He wasn't the type to be excited by rebellion or sin. He didn't *want* to be gay. And he definitely wasn't shoving any agenda in our faces.

Noah just wanted to be normal. He just wanted to be loved and accepted. He loved God and knew God loved him. But he couldn't change the way he felt, and he didn't understand why God would let him have these powerful feelings. Again, I heard his question from that night: "Why did God make me this way?"

These were the words that changed forever my perspective of what it means to be a gay person. Noah didn't want this. Noah didn't choose this. Who would choose this? Why would someone want the torment that comes with being gay—the constant rejection, the looks of disgust, a life of struggling so hard to belong, a lifetime of feeling alone. Knowing Noah shattered all my paradigms.

Chapter Two

Context

I think no parent can be fully prepared for their child's "coming out" moment. But with my background, I may have been even less prepared than the typical parent.

I became a Christian at age five and was baptized a few years later. I was raised in a conservative Baptist church with very traditional views I found so very comforting. There were rules for everything, and I loved rules. Knowing right from wrong (and being right about things) brought certainty, and I still love certainty.

I was raised going to church Sunday morning, Sunday night, Wednesday night, and extra times for church-related things like Awana. My mom was my Sunday school teacher and hosted Backyard Bible Clubs at our house for years so all the neighborhood kids could have the opportunity to come to know Jesus.

I loved it all. I loved the memory verses, the "sword drills," the nudges to do my quiet time and to put God first and glorify him in everything I did. I loved the youth group retreats I went on to get that "mountaintop high" spiritual experience.

I went to a Christian school and learned about God

throughout my education. I believed everything I was taught and never challenged anything. Not only was (and is) the Bible the inerrant Word of God, but so were the translations of it that were written and interpreted by man.

Not only was I in church three times a week and a Christian school most of the rest of it; I also spent entire summers at a Christian camp. There, I was taught three truths I would remember for the rest of my life: "dare to be different," make it the goal of my life to glorify God, and always obey his commands.

One of the key things I learned was that, apart from blasphemy, the biggest sin you could commit was homosexuality. Even from a young age I was taught to have a category for gay people. It wasn't long before I was convinced that every gay person could be characterized as loud, promiscuous, flamboyant, rainbow-flag-waving, in-your-face, and agenda-driven.

I remember secretly liking all of the songs from the band Queen, but feeling guilty any time I listened to "We Are the Champions" or "We Will Rock You," because I believed the lead singer was a sinner because he was gay.

I was taught and was certain that being gay was a choice. It was a sexual lifestyle that was clearly against God's will. Not only was it a choice, but all parents were certainly to blame for their son or daughter being gay.

By the time I went to graduate school to get my masters in professional counseling I had "the gay thing" all figured out. Gay people were so enthralled with sin that they were depraved (oh, how I loved churchy terms), and that depravity was what led them to be attracted to someone of the same sex as one of the stages of sexual addiction.

But there was a hiccup in graduate school. While completing my coursework, I learned something that poked a small hole in my certainty. A professor shared some very compelling evidence from several studies done in other countries that caused me to pause for a moment and think, *What if this isn't a choice?* He spoke of hormones that could be given to a person or an animal that could change their physical sexual attraction. It sparked my interest but really didn't have a huge impact on my beliefs.

At this point, I thought I had the perfect marriage and four perfect kids. My husband was the best, and my kids loved Jesus. They each accepted Christ at a young age, and I was relieved each was going to heaven. "The Prayer" had been prayed, so the deal was done. What more could a mother and wife ask for?

As my kids got older, some of their entertainment choices would feature gay people, and I was always annoyed that "they" were trying to push the gay agenda in our faces. I didn't even know who the "they" were. I just knew they were actively trying to lead me down "the slippery slope" until I wouldn't even be bothered if gay people were glorified on television.

I remember one of my kids' closest friends coming out. My first question was whether the person knew it was a "sin." I worried about how their parents were doing, but then quickly cast that concern aside because I was convinced it was their fault anyway. I was compassionate, but I truly believed these poor kids were running from God, and I was more concerned they would be a bad influence on my children. Then something happened, something that still horrifies and embarrasses me as I think about the judgment I passed on those poor kids and their parents.

One of these many moments of regret that still pains me today came while our family watched *American Idol*. It was Noah's favorite show, and we all loved it and watched every season.

Noah was 12 at the time, and this particular season

Adam Lambert was the contestant we were cheering for. He was a rocker and a little bit loud for me, but Noah liked him, so I did too. But then the news came out that he was gay. Apparently he had kissed a guy, and it was posted on the Internet. It went viral. What I said when I learned of his sexual orientation I can never take back, and Noah heard every word. I said, "I can't believe he is gay! That is disgusting. I don't think I like him anymore." Oh, to know that Noah heard those words and took them in! He must have thought, *Well, I might be gay. If she knows about me, I guess she will think I am disgusting and won't like me anymore.*

He heard many phrases and witnessed more than a few looks of disgust from me and my family during the years he kept his secret. It hurts that he felt anything but love from me, even though it was all unintentional and from an uneducated point of view.

A year later I met Amy when she came to work with me on staff in the Care department of the church where I work. As I mentioned before, at the time Amy was married with three kids, but she was gay. She was my first close friend that had "the struggle," as she referred to it back then. Amy is like many of my friends. She loves God and is a follower of Jesus.

We spent hours and hours talking about what it was like to be her and what she had gone through from the time she was a child until now. My empathy for her and gay people grew with each conversation, and as a result, my views about gay people began to shift. Amy wasn't loud or agenda-driven. She wasn't depraved or sexually addicted. She was married, she loved Jesus, and found her true identity in Christ. I didn't even think that was possible.

My time spent with her taught me many things, one of which was that being gay was probably not a choice. She told me she had prayed many times in her childhood for God to take her feelings away. She told me she never would have chosen her life of struggle.

Amy exposed me to so many misconceptions I had about those who are attracted to someone of the same sex. We talked for hours about what her life was like growing up, what it was like now, and how she thought about things. With each conversation, my empathy grew. I began to change. My beliefs shifted. My heart softened.

If you can't tell from what I have shared so far, my family was pretty "vanilla." I would describe us as pretty solid (whatever that means). Al and I worked hard to love each other well, our kids behaved most of the time, and we were all very involved in church. To my knowledge, even through high school, partying and experimenting with drugs, alcohol, and sex weren't really on their radar.

Whenever it was time to share a testimony or our story in our couples small group to get to know each other, I always felt guilty for how simple our lives were and how we hadn't really gone through anything significant. My testimony was so boring I was embarrassed to tell it.

As a counselor, I would listen to my clients' stories and hurt for them and empathize with them. Then I'd go home and thank God I had not gone through anything like they had.

I did go through some intense anxiety in my twenties for a period of six months. I had numerous panic attacks, generalized anxiety, and a healthy fear of dying. While that was excruciating, we eventually figured it out, and I consider it part of what made me a great counselor. It enabled me to really empathize with individuals experiencing anxiety because I had walked through it myself and made it to the other side.

But then our perfect life changed forever—for the first time. A couple years before Noah's big reveal, my daughter began struggling with depression. At 18 she was diagnosed with bipolar disorder. I was caught off guard because, as a counselor, I had always believed being bipolar was a condition of high highs and low lows. Her type of bipolar actually was characterized by an agitated state more than a high state when she was manic, so that kept me from seeing the signs.

Our precious daughter struggled hard. The family's tumultuous journey lasted at least four solid years, with her attempting suicide at least three times landing her in different hospitals for psychiatric treatment and us agonizing over trying to keep her alive.

I became a student of the disorder. That is what I do. When I go through something, I research it to death. I learned everything there was to know about the disorder, suicide, and how to love and support someone with this diagnosis.

My heart for the suicidal and for others grew and grew as I learned how to set aside judgment, speak up, and educate others about marginalized, mentally ill individuals, one of whom I now knew personally.

Those with mental illness are stigmatized greatly, and their parents are often blamed for it. And my daughter was so normal. You never would have known she struggled with anything. She didn't fit the category of someone experiencing mental illness.

Sound familiar?

Little did I know what God was preparing us for through all of this. What I learned then would eventually have the potential to save my son's life.

Chapter Three

Words of Wisdom

During those very early days after what I call "The Reveal," I turned to those who were either gay themselves or who had a heart for gay people for advice and wisdom in my search for answers. I needed help desperately, and I wanted answers from someone who also loved Jesus, living the life my son was.

I called Aaron, a guy at our church I knew to be gay who loves Jesus. I asked if he would meet with Al and me. He agreed, and a few days later we were sitting across from him in my office at the church. We were still very overwhelmed and in shock. It had only been a week since Noah's reveal.

He must have known we were in pain, because the first thing he said when he sat down was, "Noah is going to be okay. God was not surprised by this, and there is hope for Noah's future." I sobbed, my dam of tears breaking with his words of solace. My tears were tears of pain, but also of relief. He was right; God knows everything. This did not catch him by surprise.

Tears continued to flow down my face with each word he said. It was like he could see our despair and knew what we were feeling, what we were processing, and what our fears were. What a comfort those statements were, because from the second Noah told us he was gay, we couldn't help but lose some hope for our son's future. Our dreams for him were shattered, and we could no longer see anything good on the horizon for him.

He went on to describe four paths Noah could take. He could end up marrying a woman and living like my friend Amy was. I have to admit that, at the time, this was the one we hoped for most. I think many parents who learn their son or daughter is gay hope they are at least bisexual, so they can put them in the "normal" category by hiding the same sex part and seeing them marry someone of the opposite sex. Then no one has to know, and they can live a "normal" life. Parents don't want their child to have the hard life that comes with how the world treats those in same-sex relationships.

The second option Aaron outlined was that Noah could remain celibate the rest of his life, like Wesley Hill shares in his book, *Washed and Waiting*. Al and I saw that as a good option as well. It would be hard, but he could do it. Aaron was doing it, and he seemed happy.

The third option was that he could date and fall in love with a man and enter into a monogamous relationship. They could love God and practice the relationship values that straight Christian couples practice: commitment, putting God first and center in their lives, and living a life of self-sacrifice for the other. This option was disturbing and even uncomfortable for us to even think about at the time (I am ashamed to say that now, but it was how I felt). We hoped this wouldn't be the path he took.

Although we thought there were only three options for Noah to choose from, Aaron went on to explain there was a fourth option as well, one he thought to be the most likely of the four. He shared frankly that Noah could live a life filled with one-night stands with many gay men. Aaron explained this path to be the one chosen by many gay men because they cannot find acceptance anywhere else.

He went on to explain that when a gay person cannot find acceptance in faith communities, they search for it in other communities. This option saddened us the most because it meant Noah might walk away from his relationship with God. This pathway was one we hadn't thought of. We had considered the first three even before Aaron told us about them, but we had never thought about this, let alone identified it as the most likely of the four. Of course this was the path we did not want for our son more than any of the others! This could lead to so much intimacy damage, disease, and, most importantly, we didn't want to see Noah turn away from his relationship with God.

Aaron continued, "Noah needs to know he can be gay and be a Christian. Most think they can't be both. The message out there today, especially in the church, is that if you are gay God does not love you and the church and other Christians won't accept you. They'll want to change you. If Noah leaves the church over this, then we have failed as a church. We need to do everything we can to point Noah toward Jesus and not away, and remove any barriers by how we love him, what we say, and the questions we ask. Whatever we do has the potential to push Noah either away from or toward Jesus."

Al and I use this decision-making lens to this day. When we are thinking through anything that has to do with Noah, we ask ourselves, "If we do this thing or that thing, will it push Noah further away from Jesus or draw him closer?" It really clarifies the decisions we make.

Aaron went on to counsel us to invite Noah to invite God into whatever he does. "Simple decisions he makes now can have the potential to become central decisions later in his life that may have long-term consequences."

Aaron's words were dripping with wisdom we could apply that educated us on the roles we could play.

Many times as parents we just want to know what our role is in all of this. We don't want to mess this up any further. We already may have done a lot of damage as our child was growing up. Although we are often clueless about to what to do, our intentions are pure in wanting what is best for our kids.

Al and I were in this spot. We wanted so much to do the right thing, but didn't have a clue what to do, what direction to take, or what role to play.

What Aaron said next was liquid gold. It was simple counsel that would carry us for years to come and guide us on our decision-making path.

He went on to share a guiding principle he had learned from the late Reverend Billy Graham. The God we have come to know as multifaceted has three very important roles he often plays. We refer to these as the Trinity. And within those roles, he is God the father, the Holy Spirit who convicts us, and Jesus who loves us sacrificially.

When we need wisdom about what role to play in our child's life or anyone's life we are part of, it is helpful to remember Reverend Graham's words: **"It is God's job to judge, the Holy Spirit's job to convict, and our job to love."** As Jesus lives his life through us, as it is described in much of the New Testament, the role we play is the same as his—to love.

Jesus represents the key role we should focus on as parents. **Love**. Al and I need to love Noah. Jesus lives through us, so we need to allow Jesus to love Noah through us. Jesus loves with grace, acceptance, and sometimes, but less often, with truth. Al and I decided to love Noah and allow

The Big Reveal

the Holy Spirit to convict him if he sins. He has a relationship with God, so we do not have to take it upon ourselves to be the Holy Spirit.

We are to love our LGBTQ+ kids, our straight cisgender kids, our coworkers, our neighbors with this same love.

For me, loving Noah like Jesus loves means setting aside what I want to say to him about what I believe or want him to believe, so he can see Jesus through me.

Only you can know what loving your child like Jesus loves will look like. Loving your son or daughter may look like attending their wedding, not because you are condoning it, but because you love them and want them to know you are for them and desire to be an active part of their lives.

In the early days with Noah after he came out, we really didn't know what the role of Jesus's love through us would look like or require, but just knowing what that love felt like personally simplified so much for us. We walked away from that meeting with Aaron that day knowing that our role was to focus on exemplifying Jesus's love. We weren't to judge. That's God the father's role. We weren't to try to convict Noah. We could leave that intimate work to the Holy Spirit. Our main role in Noah's life was to use every opportunity to embody the love of Jesus before him.

This conversation with Aaron carried us for the next few months and parts of it still do today. God used Aaron to comfort us, to love us, to meet us where we were. And he gave us a single question to examine every decision as we interact with Noah: "Will this push Noah away from Jesus or toward Jesus?" So many things Aaron said that day set us on our path of understanding, empathizing, and healing.

I am so thankful for the wisdom Aaron shared, and we are forever grateful to God for using a gay man to impart these truths. It was a glimmer of hope that Noah could be like Aaron some day: he could continue to love Jesus and be okay.

The Talk With A Pastor

The next step in our journey was to talk with a pastor. Even though we attend and I work for an enormous church, I had the kind of relationship with my pastor that enabled me to call on him for some words of advice after this life-altering personal event. All of my concern for what others thought of me was out the window. I was so broken that I didn't even care if he knew about my son or the questions swirling in my mind.

I texted him first and just said, "Two weeks ago Noah came out to us. Is there any chance I could ask you a few questions about it?"

He responded immediately: "Call me as soon as you can."

We scheduled a phone call, and for the next 30 minutes my mind raced as I thought about what I would ask and what I would say. I wondered, *Was it a sin for Noah to like this other guy? Is a monogamous, same-sex, long-term relationship a sin?*

When I heard his voice, tears overwhelmed my words. I was able to compose myself enough to be able to ask the question that had been haunting my mind for two weeks: "Is it a sin to be gay?"

I knew I would believe his answer, whatever he said. He is very knowledgeable about the Bible, and I could trust him to tell me the truth. So I asked him that burning question. His response was one of the most healing things I've ever heard.

He was quick to ask me what I meant by my question, and I am so glad he did. He asked, "Do you mean is it a sin to be gay, or is it a sin to act on it?" I am so glad he clarified, because so many people combine the two, and I was doing that as well.

I answered, "I guess I mean to act on it."

He said, "Well, I know for sure that it is not a sin to be gay, because that is just an *is*. He can't help that he is gay, and I don't think he chose it. I have never known one to choose it in all of the gay people I have met over the years."

Okay, that makes sense, I thought. I remembered Noah asking why God had made him this way, and he had prayed for God to take it away and he hadn't. He didn't choose it. He wouldn't choose it.

I continued, "But is it a sin to act on it?"

He paused for a minute and softly said words that brought me immense relief. "I don't know. For years I thought I knew the answer to that question. But my relationships and conversations with gay men and women have softened my certainty."

A strange sensation came over me in that moment. As much as I hate uncertainty, I can't tell you how his words—"I don't know."—warmed my heart that day and continue to. I didn't know either, and that was okay. If he didn't know, it was okay that I didn't.

Our conversation continued. He shared, "Clearly the person Paul is describing in Romans 1 is not Noah. I know many gay people. I've never met a gay person who fits that description. I've met a few straight people who do!"

He continued, "If Noah feels he needs to leave the church as a result of being gay, we have failed." There it was again. Aaron had said the same thing. With even my limited experience, I knew why so many kids were leaving their faith over this. He concluded, "Our role should be to help them come to terms with things and honor God with it."

I remember a few other things he said vividly:

"It is not natural to you to be in a same-sex relationship,

but it is natural for Noah. Don't tell him it's unnatural; that is not helpful but rather hurtful and further separating, because he already does not feel normal and thinks he is disgusting to others."

"We should treat Noah as a person with an unanswered prayer. He has prayed for this to go away, and for some reason God has not allowed that. Ask yourself what does loving him look like in light of that?"

So many words of wisdom and relief had come from this man. I am still so thankful for the words he spoke that day. They were so comforting, so loving, so empathic, and life-giving, which was the opposite of what I was hearing at this point from others I had chosen to tell.

When I would venture out of my comfort zone to share vulnerably with others about Noah, most of the time my story was met with this response: "Well, I have to let you know I think it is a sin." I wasn't even asking for their position on the subject. I was just sharing something difficult that had happened in my life recently.

The journey continued as I tried to find answers to my many questions. I discovered that all my life I had worshipped certainty. I loved knowing right from wrong and considered everything black and white. Now everything in my life was gray, and it was a very uncomfortable place to be. I longed for what I had lost, but yet I was so relieved that I could be uncertain and still be okay.

Chapter Four

Write It All Down

Just like I did with my daughter's illness, I immediately tried to get my hands on everything I could read to help me know how to understand and respond to my son. I devoured every article I could find, books on the subject, people I could talk to—anything! I was still in the dark, with only the words my pastor and Aaron gave me to say and not a clue what to do. I needed help, and I needed it fast.

In most Christian circles, a son or daughter coming out is not good news. Because of this, no one talks about it. We felt very alone, like there was nowhere to turn to get answers. So I began writing down everything I was learning in hopes it would help someone else. I hoped someone might even be able to know this ahead of time, rather than learn it in desperation like I had to. I wrote it all down for *me* to remember too. I didn't want to lose anything I had learned. I didn't want to miss anything. I wanted to cement it all in my mind so I would know what to do at all times. I couldn't afford to make any more mistakes with Noah. I had already made so many.

I wrote basic lessons, and I wrote lessons that would take up a whole chapter.

Debbie Causey

FOUR BASIC LESSONS I WROTE TO MYSELF

1. Flip out on the inside, not the outside. Remember this as you find out new things about your LGBTQ+ son or daughter. Remain calm and loving on the outside. Doing so is actually critical. It may be too late for the initial reveal if you are reading this right now and your son or daughter has already come out, but it is never too late to begin responding calmly and lovingly, and to accept other things they will tell you in the future. The hope is that they will tell you more. Your child needs to know your love for them will not change as a result of anything they will tell you.

As I mentioned, when my son came out I was immediately nauseous to the point where I thought I would throw up. Not because I was disgusted by the news, but because the stress of the reveal was so intense that it made me very ill. Can you imagine if I had thrown up? It could have confirmed to Noah in his mind that I really did think he was disgusting, so disgusting that I even threw up.

How you respond to their reveal has the potential to determine how they think you feel about them, how they think God feels about them, and if they believe they have a future. Imagine the courage it took to tell you about their sexual orientation or gender identity especially if they feared your response based on your beliefs. In the moment they reveal to you their reality, they are usually filled with so much doubt, fear, guilt, shame, and intense emotions. Recognize what it took for them to tell you, and meet them in that moment with what they need the most, unconditional love and acceptance. Let them know you are so glad that they told you.

They need to hear things like, "I love you. I am here for you. You do not need to walk this alone."

By the time your child has come out to you, more than

likely they have already come to terms with it. They have been grappling with it, possibly for years, and are used to it, so to speak. They have already asked the questions, felt the feelings, gone through the denial, anger, shame, etc. Many try to date someone of the opposite gender to try to prove to themselves that they can form an attraction. My son tried and failed.

The only problem is that they are more than likely expecting you to be in the same place they are when they decide it's time to tell you. There is not a lot of wiggle room for you to grieve openly to your child at that point without it seeming like you don't love them anymore. You do need to work through the myriad of emotions, but you will need to find support from others to be able to do this. Your child cannot and should not be your support as you go through this. They cannot be that for you emotionally. Give yourself time to process all of your own emotions. Be kind to yourself and your child as you go through this time.

Try not to ask them if they are sure. Everyone in my family assumed Noah was going through a phase. The child assumes this too. They've been walking through that phase without you, perhaps for years. Unfortunately, coming out as gay, lesbian, bisexual, or even transgender is not a normal phase of development and is more than likely not a phase for your son or daughter. Many times we believe it to be a phase because we're grasping for our hope of the "normal life" we want to believe is possible for our child.

While The Reveal is scary for you, part of remaining calm on the outside is realizing they were probably scared to death to tell you. So many parents have handled the news terribly and have kicked their son or daughter out of their house, stopped paying for college, declared them to be an abomination, or worse yet, led them to believe they were going to hell. Your loved one has heard many of these stories and has created some scenario in their mind of how you will respond. If they tell you, they are doing so because they have decided they are strong enough to bear the consequences, or because they can't keep it from you any longer. How you choose to respond in that moment will determine whether they will regret telling you.

2. Your child did not choose this. Some of Noah's first words were "Why did God make me this way?" and "I have prayed for him to take this away, and he won't."

As you consider what you've been told, ask yourself, "Who would choose this?" Initially most gay people would say they don't want it, and if given the chance they would change it if they could. Author Andrew Marin says in his book, *Us vs. Us*, that 96% of LGBTQ+ individuals have prayed for God to take this reality away, whether they are Christian or not.

This means there are even LGBTQ+ atheists out there who have prayed to a god they don't believe in out of a desire to change their sexual orientation or gender identity in the hopes their prayer would be answered.

Not only did they not choose this, but some studies show that adolescents recognize their first attraction to the same sex sometime between ages 10 and 15. Yet the average age a child comes out to their parents is 17 years of age (Marin 2016 p.131). Noah silently wrestled with his attraction for at least four excruciating years before telling us. Your child has probably been dealing with this much longer than you realize.

What is wrong with praying for my child to be straight or to be the gender they were assigned at birth? At least two well-known authors claim to be straight when they were once gay. They attribute this reality to God, and I do not deny the possibility. For all things are possible with God.

The problem is that there are millions more who have

prayed to be straight or for God to change their gender identity, and God has not performed this transformation. The reason such testimonials can be harmful is the many for whom this is not their experience hear the story of transformation and try and fail to pray away their unwanted attraction or gender identity. They end up taking on the blame and often try to harm themselves because they believe they are not good enough for God to do this for them or that God must not love them. This can spiral into self-loathing, shame, and other harm that can add to the suffering your child is already experiencing. If we are not careful, they could hold themselves to the same concepts that are taught in the no longer recommended conversion therapy, also known as reparative therapy, which can actually traumatize your child, adding to the shame and self-hatred they are feeling.

3. You did not cause this! As a younger Christian who was taught that homosexuality is a sin, I believed the parents were to blame when a son or daughter came out as LGBTQ+. I believed the child's sexual orientation was a result of an overbearing mom and a disengaged dad or trauma somewhere in someone's past. After looking at most of the research available and concluding that there is no definitive evidence to support this theory, I still feel enormous pain at the thought that there might be a minute chance I caused this hard life to come to my child.

Although the research does not confirm it, many people still believe it. We have family members who believe it and told us so regularly.

There are many gay individuals who had great childhoods with great parents and no trauma, and many straight kids with traumatic childhoods and overbearing and disengaged parents who are not gay. Many parents can attest to the fact that they saw signs of their son or daughter being gay or transgender from the very early years without there being any trauma.

Thinking you are the cause can be among the most painful emotions you can experience, though, and you need to work through and heal from it. There are still so many Christians who believe it is your fault that your son or daughter is LGBTQ+. They might be wrong, but that doesn't make it hurt less.

You may need to work with a counselor to get through the depression or anxiety you are experiencing as a result of coming out of the closet (or you going in) after your son or daughter came out. Even though I am a counselor, I worked with one as I processed my son being gay and what that would mean for him and our family. It was so helpful.

4. Being LGBTQ+ does not go hand-in-hand with a sinful lifestyle. Just because your son or daughter is gay or transgender doesn't mean they are being promiscuous or "living the lifestyle." For me, understanding this came easily because Noah was such a straight-laced kid from birth. He wasn't sleeping around, using substances or behaving in ways often attached to being gay. For many, many parents this is not their experience, and I realize I didn't do anything special to have this luxury. I am so grateful. In many if not most situations, LGBTQ+ individuals act out in sinful ways at the same time they come out, whether they are sleeping around, drinking, using drugs, or running from Christianity in every possible way. Many times this allows parents to consider all these behaviors part of being LGBTQ+. It is not surprising that most LGBTQ+ individuals turn to these forms of coping, given what they are going through, or to a community of people doing these things because with them they are accepted for who they are.

Noah didn't really act out in this way by participating in sinful behaviors that usually accompany someone running from God. Even though he was struggling with immense shame and longed to belong to a community that accepted him, Noah's morality, which stemmed from his relationship with Jesus and his commitment to follow him, made it much easier for me to be able to separate Noah being gay from the sins he commits. It allowed me to see that Noah being gay did not necessarily bring with it those other sins.

That isn't to say that there is not hyper-sexuality and a lot of promiscuity in some of the LGBTQ+ culture. But this also characterizes straight culture today. I know gay married couples with incredibly strong faith that live very moral lives and straight couples having affairs for whom immorality plagues their relationship. Overall, what brought me comfort was that one didn't necessarily mean the other would be present. As parents, we could benefit from learning to separate the two.

Christians also need to separate the two. So many times people do not even realize they have lumped the two together. This is understandable, since most who are turning from God because of the rejection they have felt for years are running to these coping behaviors, but that doesn't make it true for all who identify as gay or transgender. It is important to separate the two so the problem areas of sin can be addressed, rather than speaking against their identity, which they believe is a huge part of who they are. Refusing to separate behavior from identity can complicate your relationship and encourage them to turn to other coping strategies and not to you when they are going through something hard. If we offer unconditional love and acceptance, they will feel safer to turn to us when they are in need.

References:

Marin, Andrew, *Us vs. Us.*

Chapter Five

Empathy Grows

It wasn't until I replayed some of my son's past and considered what he must have experienced in childhood and adolescence as he grew up in our family that my empathy for him and the LGBTQ+ community skyrocketed. My heart broke as I remembered conversation after conversation and experience after experience where we communicated how unacceptable being gay was to us. It was communicated verbally and nonverbally to Noah, who absorbed the pain and fears that came from them.

If you haven't taken this journey yourself, imagine if you can what it's like for a young gay or transgender person growing up in a religious home.

Think about being five or six years old. Your friends are talking about baby dolls or sports, and you are drawn to the activities the opposite sex enjoys. It isn't long before you start to realize boys are supposed to love sports and girls are supposed to love dolls, and if you love the opposite of what you are supposed to, your parents show a little disappointment or even express concern with your choice. You experience a little embarrassment and need to please your parents, so they will not be disappointed in you again.

Imagine you are 10 or 11. You begin to notice your friends are talking about feelings they are having for the opposite sex, and you find yourself alarmingly neutral on the subject. You wonder when you are going to experience these feelings your friends are beginning to have. You think to yourself, *Why am I feeling what they are talking about for the same sex?* You wonder when these feelings are going to go away and what you'll do if they don't.

Maybe you understand the language at this point and maybe you don't, but you have fear beginning to build inside of you for what you are experiencing. You wonder, *Am I gay? Is that what is going on inside of me?*

Maybe you come from a faith background and are entering adolescence, and you realize you haven't prayed yet for God to take this away. You begin to pray every night for God to take these feelings for the same sex away. You pray and pray and believe that if it is true that being gay is a sin, he will surely do what you ask. And yet when you wake up in the morning nothing has changed.

Then you enter high school and decide you are going to make yourself like a person of the opposite sex. You try dating for a while, and it goes pretty well until it is time to hold hands or have your first kiss. You realize you feel no spark when you do, and yet you look at your friends of the same sex and the spark is there. You feel shame for those feelings and press on to change. You may even date someone for years, hoping the feelings will change, only to find out they don't.

At church you hear phrases like "an abomination" to describe what you feel. You hear jokes about being gay, and as you experience deeper shame connected to something you know you cannot control, you decide one thing for sure—you will never tell anyone you are gay.

Everything you think from that point on is evaluated

and judged by whether it needs to be filtered, rejected as unacceptable, feelings one should not have, or words that can't be spoken so no one will know. You begin to live a double life. The hidden one inside of you and the other you allow everyone to see. Lying, hiding, and repressing become daily, if not hourly habits. Shame and emotional pain grow, even as you shove it down. You begin to become numb to rejection, numb to feelings, numb to others and how they see you. You are used to the duplicitous life you have to live, but the tension of living this way continues to build.

When you can't maintain the duplicity or manage the pain any longer it eventually comes out. You have decided you must figure out how to live your life being gay and not be rejected by everyone around you, especially by those closest to you. You can't take it anymore, and you take the risk of coming out. The proverbial dominos fall, and you search for clues from your loved ones: Are they going to accept you or reject you? Then you go for it.

As I think about this path that an LGBTQ+ person goes through from their earliest years it brings tears to my eyes. When I think about the strong possibility that my own son went through this, it breaks my heart. The coming out process is traumatic enough for so many kids, especially if their parents do not handle it well. But when you add to it the years of doubt, confusion, and loneliness prior to it, it is unbelievable that any kid could navigate it.

As a parent, I thought we handled the coming out of our son really well. Secretly, I was a little proud of us, even though we would have failed miserably had we not received good training (as pastors) on the subject two weeks prior. Even though inside we were terrified, we felt we said the right things, did the right things, and communicated nothing but love to Noah from the moment he came out. We knew we had made mistakes here and there, but for the most part we perceived The Reveal to be as damage-free as possible. So I thought it would be easy for Noah to trust us and stop living the duplicitous life he had become accustomed to. I was so wrong.

I remember driving in the car on the way to church with Noah about a month after he came out. I had made a rule with him that we would talk for 10 minutes every week on our way to church, even though the drive was 45, so he could help me get to know the part of him he'd kept secret the previous four years. We could talk about whatever he wanted, but it couldn't be small talk. It had to go beyond surface level conversation. It could be about faith, being gay, friendships, his relationship with us, or even politics. Whatever he wanted. I thought it would be a good way to get to know the Noah I didn't know. Well, he HATED it.

At the time I honestly couldn't understand why. Many times I would dissolve in tears at the end of the 10 minutes because I didn't know why he didn't want to talk to me. More upsetting was my impression that he didn't feel safe talking with me.

I prodded and prodded, trying to get him to talk, to tell me why the conversations were so hard for him and why he didn't want to have them.

Finally one Sunday he broke. "Mom, it is like you're telling me that the spider I have been told for years will bite me is now safe and won't bite me any longer. You can't just erase years of conditioning that something is unsafe and think it can all of a sudden be safe. You trained me to be scared of your reaction to gay people. Just because you've changed your perspective and how you feel doesn't mean I feel safe to talk to you now." His words pierced like a knife.

Instantly I understood. All of my verbal and nonverbal rejection of gay people, as well as the opinions I expressed about homosexuality in general through the years had conditioned Noah to think it was extremely unsafe to talk about homosexuality or admit to being gay. I could not expect him to flip a switch and suddenly believe I was a safe person now, no matter how much I wanted him to and no matter how much I tried to show him I had changed. It was going to take time. A lot of it.

I share all this to encourage you to hang in there. It will take some time to rebuild trust. It took a year for Noah to see that my new perspective of him was real and could be trusted. Today he knows I love him, that I am for him, and most of the time he does not distrust what I say. We are eight years in, and he now trusts me as a safe person to talk to. He understands my love for him. He still does not like to talk about anything deep with me or his family, but he knows if he needs us, we will be there. It took consistent conversation for him to see this.

Not all LGBTQ+ people are like Noah. I hear many stories of children who are LGBTQ+ who love to talk to their parents about their experience being gay or transgender and wish they would ask them more about it. They love to tell their stories, and at times I am envious of that kind of parent-child relationship. I wish Noah would want to tell me more about his life.

He still carries an incredible amount of shame and is in therapy for it. I imagine it will take years to undo some of the damage that was done over the years, and I grieve that every day. He is on the path to recovery to become the person he is meant to be.

Among all the good that has come from our experience is the privilege I have of expressing my love to many gay and transgender people as I listen to them tell their stories. They often say they wish their parents loved them the way I do. While it doesn't replace my desire to have stories shared from my own son, I am grateful I can be the kind of parent other LGBTQ+ individuals need and long for. I love the experiences I get to have with each and every person who has crossed my path, and I am intentional about keeping them in my life. I am better for their influence, and they have taught me so many things about how to truly love and accept everyone, even the hard-to-love people in my life.

I read this letter on Facebook from a friend of a friend to his younger self. It inspired me to look at things from a different perspective. He wrote:

Dear Timmy,

For a good portion of your life you're going to struggle with feeling like you belong...with feeling loved and accepted... you'll fear being rejected and struggle to accept the labels people put on you (including macho, appropriately on a crop top).

Your faith will sustain you but will also cause you a tremendous amount of conflict and pain as you struggle to understand and accept that the God who created you loves you and affirms you just as you are. The church, for the most part, will tell you otherwise. You're going to have your faith tested, your heart broken, and you're going to need some therapy to undo the reparative therapy you put yourself through for 8+ years trying to fix something that wasn't broken in the first place. You're going to be made fun of and misunderstood. You're going to go through periods of time where you hate yourself and wonder why you exist. You'll lose jobs and opportunities, including giving up what you think (at the time) is your dream job...all because you're struggling to accept yourself as a gay man who also wants to hold on to his faith. With no college degree, you'll make it out of that small town, and in Chicago will have the courage to speak your truth and truly embrace all of who you are.

And later, you will end up living an amazing life in New York City. Its hard to imagine, but it will happen. It's going to take you some time to wrestle your demons and to see the beauty that's truly inside of you ... you're gay, yes, but there's so much more to who you are. Be you. All of the things that make you who you are...your quirks, obsessions, passions, and things that people may say aren't normal, are things to be celebrated.

It does get better. Just have courage and keep smiling.
Love,

A much older and wiser Tim (Facebook Post by Tim Schrader)

If you haven't done so, I encourage you to walk the path of empathy by looking at your son or daughter's past from their perspective. It can show you so much and help you better understand them and love them. It might also foster healing for your son or daughter, because many times that is where empathy leads.

Chapter Six

The Suicide Rate is Real

Receiving a call or text that someone you love is tired of living this life and is thinking everyone would be better off without them is a harsh reality for so many.

My daughter with bipolar disorder used to say, "Mom, it isn't working. I have tried and tried and I am miserable. Why can't I just go home and be with Jesus? This life is hopeless and not for me."

Words don't come to you in those moments. Instead, you wonder, *How did we get here? How do I make this child I love and adore see that the world would not be a better place without them?* You so desire to express how devastated you would be if that were so and how you would miss them forever.

With the symptoms of my daughter's mental illness, I became familiar with the grip suicidal thoughts can have on an individual. What I didn't realize was so many of our LGBTQ+ kids are at greater risk for suicidal thoughts and attempts and mental health issues.

Because I am a licensed counselor, I am always interested in and concerned about statistics on mental health and suicide. But because I am a mother of an LGBTQ+ son, I am regularly fearful of them. Here are just a few to consider.

Our LGBTQ+ children are twice as likely to have a mental health condition than heterosexual individuals, especially anxiety and depression. In fact, 28% of LGBTQ+ youth and 40% of transgender youth reported feeling depressed most of the time, compared to 12% of non-LGBTQ youth. (HRC Foundation 2017)

One in three LGBTQ+ adults experience mental illness compared with one in five non-LGBTQ+ adults. (Medley 2016). Forty percent of transgender adults report serious psychological distress (e.g., suicidal ideation and attempts), compared with 5% of the general U.S. population.(James 2016)

Lesbian, gay, and bisexual adults are nearly twice as likely as heterosexual adults to experience a substance use disorder often used to cope with mental health issues or as self-medication. (Medley 2016) Transgender individuals are almost four times as likely as cisgender individuals to experience a substance use disorder. (Wanta, et al. 2019)

Alarmingly, lesbian, gay, and bisexual individuals are twice as likely to feel suicidal and more than four times as likely to attempt suicide, and 43% of transgender individuals have attempted suicide in their lifetime. (Kann 2016)

These numbers are terrifying to a parent. Believe me I know. But the reasons why are what is more concerning. There are so many reasons for these statistics, such as childhood trauma they experience because they are different from everyone else, or the rejection from parents and friends, or the hate experienced from so many. A 2019 National School Climate survey showed that 86% of LGBTQ+ youth reported being harassed or assaulted at school.

The LGBTQ+ community faces many forms of discrimination, including labeling, stereotyping, denial of opportunities or access, and verbal, mental, and physical abuse. They are one of the most targeted communities by perpetrators of hate crimes in the country.

I don't think we realize how important acceptance and belonging really are for everyone, especially for a group of people not used to getting them. Two out of three families are not offering acceptance to their child when they come out, and many are kicking their children out of their houses. An LGBTQ+ individual has a 120% higher risk of experiencing homelessness, often as a result of family rejection.

I could go on and on, and we would all be in a depressed pit by the statistics if we weren't there already. At the end of the day, what we really need to know and accept is that their lives are at risk, and we can do a lot to change that. Acceptance and belonging are the first places to start.

However, we may need to set aside the opinions of our pastors, our church friends, or our extended family for the sake of our son's or daughter's well-being. Their mental health is critical.

That is why it's so important not to do or say anything that could be perceived by them as more rejection. They are fragile, no matter how strong they appear. Sometimes those who seem strongest are those who attempt suicide.

Try to keep your eye on behaviors that are destructive, rather than using identity phrases, like referring to their "gay lifestyle" or telling them that they are sinning by using pronouns for themselves opposite of what they were assigned at birth. Making these kinds of statements could cause their mental health to be even less stable. When they act out or choose undesirable behavior, it's helpful to tell yourself they are not a bad person and that it is not because they are LGBTQ+, but they more than likely using this as a coping strategy.

I have often wondered whether there is a correlation

between being strictly an LGBTQ+ individual and having mental health issues, especially depression and anxiety, or if they are a result of growing up LGBTQ+. Many Christians and parents think about this too. And while this might be a reality, there is just as likely a chance there is no correlation. But if there is a correlation, which comes first? Some people think being gay or transgender is a mental health condition, and that anxiety, depression, and other mental health issues accompany the condition. Others think LGBTQ+ individuals are depressed and anxious because they have gone through life as a gay or transgender person and the overwhelming nature of their experience has resulted in anxiety and depression. This is what I have seen.

Many LGBTQ+ individuals did not suffer with anxiety and depression as children. Noah never did. He was so happy and carefree until he was 17. Right after he came out he experienced a depression that scared me to death. I will never forget that season, because it started when he came home from school sick one day. I asked him what was wrong, and he said his stomach hurt. He later revealed to me that his friend's mother had called him and her gay son an abomination. Noah went on to tell me that she had also told her son she would rather he be a drug addict than be gay. Noah's friend had relayed all of this to him and he was trying to digest it. As a result, Noah became very nauseous and checked out of school to come home. It wasn't long before he spiraled into a deep depression. That Thanksgiving he didn't eat a thing. He was so numb he did not put two words together the entire day. It seemed like the longest day of our lives. My worry intensified because of our family history with our daughter's illness. I thought, *Here we go again.*

He was showing all the signs of suicidal ideation, with which were already all too familiar. I was sick with concern and didn't know what to do. This lasted several days until I could get Noah an appointment to see a psychologist. His mental health journey began that day and continues today.

Many LGBTQ+ individuals describe having mental health issues as a result of what they have experienced. Many times they turn to drugs and alcohol to cope with the stress of keeping the secret of their sexual orientation or gender identity, of anticipating how their family and friends will react to their news, or of being bullied or made fun of by their peers. We do not need to know which comes first because they need extra support psychologically for the life they have ahead.

Because your child is burdened with so many things, you may need to be as supportive emotionally as they will allow you to, at least for a while. This is a great way to love them well.

But don't be surprised if your mental health takes a hit during this process. Many parents find themselves deeply depressed or anxious after their son or daughter comes out. The news can take an enormous toll on us as we worry about our child's new reality, what others will think, and are concerned about what this means for them spiritually, emotionally, physically, and psychologically.

Unfortunately, if at all possible we cannot allow our child to see that struggle. They cannot take on the responsibility for our mental health in addition to their own. That burden is too large for them to carry, and it adds to their shame and guilt. Your child has so much to navigate, including the world around them, their own confusion and the unanswered questions they have.

Turn to a counselor or a close, safe friend during this time to process what is happening to you. Process the shattered dreams you had for your child and the grief that comes too. Work through anger you might be experiencing because you now have a different life than you might have chosen for yourself. No matter what, just remember you also need support for this critical time.

References:

Sexual Orientation and Estimates of Adult Substance Use and Mental Health: Results from the 2015 National Survey on Drug Use and Health Medley, G., Lipari, R. N., Bose, J., Cribb, D. S., Kroutil, L. A., & McHenry, G. (2016, October).

Wanta, et al. "Mental Health Diagnoses Among Transgender Patients in the Clinical Setting: An All-Payer Electronic Health Record Study." Transgender Health, 4.1, 2019.

Price-Feeney et al. "Understanding the Mental Health of Transgender and Nonbinary." Journal of Adolescent Health | Volume 66, ISSUE 6, P684-690, January, 2020.

Park, H. and Mykhyalyshyn, L. "L.G.B.T. People Are More Likely to Be Targets of Hate Crimes Than Any Other Minority Group." June, 2016.

Sources: Federal Bureau of Investigation; socialexplorer.com; Census Bureau; Pew Research Center; Williams Institute

Human Rights Campaign Foundation and researchers at the University of Connecticut. "Growing Up LGBT in America." 2017

Kosciw, J. G. et al, "The 2019 National School Climate Survey: The experiences of lesbian, gay, bisexual, transgender, and queer youth in our nation's schools." New York: GLSEN. 2020

Kann, L. et al. "Youth risk behavior surveillance." MMWR Surveill Summ. 2018; 67: 1-114.

Chapter Seven

This Can Shake Their Faith

A massive study out of Chicago conducted by the Marin Foundation surveyed LGBTQ+ individuals about their personal faith and their involvement in a faith community. The results were astounding. They found that 86% were raised in a faith community from 0 to 18. More alarmingly, they found that 54% of those kids had left their religious community after the age of 18, more than double the average.

Unfortunately, we need not be surprised if our child follows the same path at some point. They might not admit this until later, but your child may have a faith crisis because they are LGBTQ+. Why?

I was sure that the night Noah revealed to us that he was gay would be the hardest news we would ever receive as parents. My dreams were shattered in that moment for what I had defined as the only healthy and successful future he could have.

My body reeled with pain as he spoke to me about being gay. Little did I know there was something more painful he could share that would cause me to long for a return to what I knew before it was revealed.

About a year after Noah came out, Al and I were out to

dinner with him while he was home for a visit from college. It was just the three of us, which I loved and cherished because of the special alone time with our youngest of four.

For my extremely introverted and "no attention on me" son, these times were tense and fear-filled as he anticipated what questions we might ask or what deep truths we might want him to share. We didn't know the extraordinary energy it took for him to even be present in what we thought of as an everyday interaction.

Near the end of that dinner I decided to ask Noah to give me a present for my upcoming birthday. I thought he would love the suggestion because it was free and simple. Little did I know that the gift I asked for would soon become the last thing I ever wanted.

"Noah, could you give me 10 minutes of telling me how you are doing spiritually? You can share whatever you want and guide the conversation wherever you want it to go." I waited excitedly for his answer.

He looked at me as though he were going to throw up but remained silent. Although he had lived away from us while at school, I still thought I knew him well enough to know when he was keeping a great secret. I had no idea what it was.

Unfortunately, I do not have the personality or the patience as a parent to allow questions to go unanswered and secrets to remain hidden. I prodded and prodded with questions for more than 15 minutes until Noah finally broke into tears and said, "I guess I don't believe in God anymore." As he sobbed, I gathered him into my arms and led him quickly out of the restaurant and into our SUV while Al stayed behind to pay the bill.

Noah was crying so hard that Al didn't miss anything because he couldn't get the words out. I held him in the back seat and just continued to rub his hair and reassure him that everything was going to be alright.

When he was finally able to talk, he said, "I have been more scared to tell you and dad this than I was when I came out. I know how important my faith is to you both, and I don't want to hurt you. You have shared with me that we could handle anything that comes along the way, as long as we have Jesus. Nothing is as important as that."

He continued, "I knew telling you this would be equal to telling you that I have cancer that is terminal, because I know you will fear my eternity after I die."

He was right! The truths he shared stabbed me in the heart and gut, and the first thing I felt was panic. I knew I couldn't show him that. This was hard for him to share, and I didn't want to make it worse.

He kept saying, "I don't want to hurt you. I love you, and I really don't want you to have pain because of me."

I don't know how I did this, but I controlled myself and told him it was all going to be okay. He didn't need to be afraid. We loved him no matter what, and he didn't have to worry about hurting us.

Oddly enough, his worry of hurting us gave me comfort, because it allowed me to hope that the Holy Spirit was still inside of him because he was showing the fruits of the Spirit (love, kindness, goodness). I hoped that Jesus was still in him, because I didn't know how he would be so concerned about us otherwise.

That hope did not take away the pain of the news I felt then. It was devastating, and I spent much of the next week crying alone in my bedroom. I felt so hopeless, so worried, and so fearful of all this revelation meant. Noah telling me he was gay seemed so minuscule compared to this.

What I wouldn't give to go back to knowing Noah only as gay! I couldn't think of anything else. The obsessive thoughts started again, but instead of hearing "Noah is gay. My son is gay," even though I don't believe you can lose your salvation, I couldn't stop the new words that echoed in my head and heart: "Noah isn't a Christian. Noah is not going to heaven when he dies. Noah doesn't believe." It became the only thing that mattered to Al and me.

My son wasn't the only one experiencing a crisis of faith. My crisis of faith was soon to come. My disappointment with God for allowing Noah to turn from his faith caused me to fall into a deep depression. I couldn't understand why he would allow Noah to be gay, the very thing that caused Noah to question God's goodness and ultimately keep him from relationship with him. I knew God could change it in a moment or reveal himself to him through an experience that Noah could not mistake as divine intervention. Why didn't he? Why would God allow him to experience something Noah had prayed he would take away, something that would cause him to be rejected by others, when acceptance was the very thing he craved? I found myself in a cynical place. I told myself, "Well, God sacrificed his own son, why wouldn't he sacrifice mine?" I was not willing to do that.

Why is what Noah told us at that fateful dinner happening to so many LGBTQ+ individuals who grew up in religious homes? Why are 54% of those who were raised in a faith community leaving it? I had to know the answer and do something to make it stop.

The Chicago study reported that the number one reason many participants gave for leaving the faith was a negative personal experience. They didn't stop believing in God because they had hard questions that couldn't be answered, but because they had a bad experience with God and/or the church.

If you are a parent of an LGBTQ+ child, there is a good chance your child is struggling with their faith, is questioning their faith, or has left the faith. Your child may be wondering if God even exists or, if he does, if he is loving and good.

Many conclude he is not. Remember, they have left their faith because of a negative experience and often blame God for that negative experience. This can take the form of an unanswered prayer. They may have prayed for God to take their gay away or asked him to change their gender identity and he hasn't. It is very natural and normal for your son or daughter to go through this.

Noah is going through this even now. As much as I understand how he has come to his conclusion about God and faith, it is very painful to see the distance between him and God. And the worst part is I have absolutely no control over it. Above all else, the one thing Al and I have always wanted for our children is that they have a personal relationship with Jesus. It is difficult for me to go through each day knowing he has turned away from that relationship.

We can feel helpless or even devastated at times because of where our kids are in their faith journeys. Over the years we have tried to give our kids a faith of their own, and for some of us what we may feel about their walking away from their church or their beliefs pales in comparison to the terrifying prospect that they may be walking away from their eternity.

This fear and concern can become so great that we can react in ways that are not helpful. It is really difficult not to try to control their journey. As they were growing up, we had a great deal of control over what they said and did. As they get older, that authority lessens. What we end up with as they become adults is a relationship with very little control but the opportunity for an incredible amount of influence. When our kids are adults, our only job is to influence.

I learned early on that we gain this influence with our children very, very slowly, but it accrues over time. As slowly as we earn it, with one wrong comment or through one bad situation we can lose it instantaneously. This could push them farther away from God in the process.

We become safe parents when we let them ask their questions, express their doubts, and declare their unbelief. They need this process to grow a faith of their own that has not been handed to them by us. For many LGBTQ+ individuals, that might mean they need to be given the time necessary to learn to trust us, God, or the church again after their negative experience. This may involve allowing them to walk away from their faith to find a faith of their own, no matter how long that takes. This is incredibly difficult and scary, but the safety we exhibit for them in this process might allow us to be a bridge, not a barrier, to their return or to a renewed exploration of their faith. According to the Marin Foundation study, 76% of the individuals surveyed who have walked away from their faith said they are willing to return to it, compared to 9% of average Americans.

But how do we become the safest people for our LGBTQ+ children? What does that require of us? While you might think it is knowing your theology, providing information, or answering their hard questions, you would be wrong.

A friend and colleague who worked in a ministry designed to create an environment where people could seek answers to their faith questions shared some truths with me that have impacted my life to this day. The truths he shared have allowed me to understand some of what Noah is going through and what he needs from me during this phase of his spiritual journey. Adam gave me some hope for a future relationship between God and my son.

Adam explained to me that any person who is struggling with their faith, questioning faith, or who has left because of a bad experience needs a Christian to be a **demonstration** of faith and love to them. He warned me that ***"our demonstration of faith better be better than our explanation of faith."*** You may want to read that again.

This is of the utmost importance because our children aren't struggling with their faith or leaving their faith because it has failed them intellectually. They are leaving because it has failed them emotionally. They've had a bad personal experience. They were rejected. They felt unloved or that they did not belong. Adam counseled me with this fact: **"You can't 'logic' someone into something they 'emotioned' their way out of."**

Instead of looking at their struggle with faith like they need good answers to hard questions about Jesus, consider what they may need to heal from these difficult experiences. We need to enable that healing. The best way for me to allow my children to heal is to become someone they can trust. Only then will I have the influence I desire.

In the book, *I Once Was Lost*, authors Don Everts and Doug Schaupp describe a person's journey to becoming a Christian. They describe five thresholds that a person walks through along the way to accepting Christ. These five thresholds are not circumstances anyone has control over, but doorways each person walks through as they move toward becoming a Christian. The first one is trusting a Christian. In order for anyone to come to Christ, they have to experience knowing a Christian they trust.

That's troubling because most LGBTQ+ individuals do not trust Christians because of the bad experience they had that caused them to leave their faith community. So what can we do? What does it look like to be trustworthy? I am still learning to turn this over to God and ask him to reveal to me what part I am to play in this in Noah's life. As easy as this sounds, it could be the hardest aspect of control to relinquish.

The apostle Paul gives us great advice about how to

be a Christian worth trusting. In Galatians 5:6 he states, "The only thing that counts is faith expressing itself through love." Our kids need expressions of our love more than anything. As Adam said, **our demonstration of faith better be better than our explanation of faith.** And what does a demonstration of faith look like? Once again Paul has the answer in I Corinthians 13. Love is defined as patient, kind, not keeping a record of wrongs, always persevering, always protecting, always trusting, always hoping.

We need to be parents who live love to our kids. Living love looks so different to me now. I used to have a really hard time loving all people, especially those in the LGBTQ+ community. One specific example of this was what I used to think of those who participated in the Pride parade. I used to think "these people" were sinful and were trying to shove their agenda in my face. I was so appalled at even the thought of this event. I would even go as far as to say I thought their display was disgusting. But then Noah came out, and I decided to attend. I ended up going by myself, and the experience was an emotional roller coaster.

Atlanta has a huge parade with thousands lining the streets. As I got off mass transit and began to walk up the street a very short distance to the center of the parade, I could hear hateful words coming from a megaphone. I discovered the horrible, hateful things were being chanted by members of a church who often frequent these parades. What they said isn't even worth repeating. It is unloving and not of God. That day, I realized those words weren't only being shouted about the LGBTQ+ community. Those words were being shouted about my son. It was more than I could bear.

Standing amongst thousands of people, I began to sob. I had no one to talk to and nowhere to turn. I remembered my friend Aaron was going to be there, and I texted him my location. He met me where I was and I ugly cried on his chest for a good 10 minutes. He made sure I was okay and left to meet his party at another location of the parade.

I wasn't even sure why I was crying. I was experiencing more emotions in that moment than I could name. I was angry with the hateful church members for what they were chanting about my son and the many others I was growing to love. I was lonely because I had no one with whom to experience this monumental event. I was hurt because I longed for my son to be with me at the parade. But most of all I was full of love for every person walking in that parade. I had a completely different understanding of them now.

Instead of seeing people as disgustingly dressed (or undressed) who were trying to shove their agendas in my face, all I could see now were people to be loved. They just wanted to be loved. Even the loudest, crudest individuals in the parade really just wanted to be loved and accepted. Many of them have just given up on trying to get it in passive ways and have decided to walk out of the shame they have felt their whole lives and embrace their identity and not be afraid of the consequences any longer.

When I was reading the book *Us vs. Us* by Andrew Marin, I came across this story that reminded me of my experience at the parade, and it moved me to tears. This is what Nathan Albert, the dressed person in the picture, shared.

Debbie Causey

Pride Parade Hug – *Us vs. Us*

"I spent the day at Chicago's Pride Parade. Some friends and I, with The Marin Foundation, wore shirts with 'I'm Sorry' written on it. We had signs that said, 'I'm sorry that Christians judge you,' 'I'm sorry the way churches have treated you,' 'I used to be a bible-banging homophobe, sorry.' We wanted to be an alternative Christian voice from the protestors that were there speaking hate into megaphones. What I loved most about the day is when people 'got it.' I loved watching people's faces as they saw our shirts, read the signs, and looked back at us. Responses were incredible. Some people blew us kisses, some hugged us, some screamed thank you. A couple ladies walked up and said we were the best thing they had seen all day. I wish I had counted how many

people hugged me. One guy in particular softly said, 'Well, I forgive you.'

Watching people recognize our apology brought me to tears many times. It was reconciliation personified. My favorite though was a gentleman who was dancing on a float. He was dressed solely in white underwear and had a pack of abs like no one else. As he was dancing on the float, he noticed us and jokingly yelled, 'What are you sorry for? It's pride!' I pointed to our signs and watched him read them. Then it clicked. Then he got it.

He stopped dancing. He looked at all of us standing there. A look of utter seriousness came across his face. And as the float passed us he jumped off of it and ran towards us. In all his sweaty beautiful abs of steel, he hugged me and whispered, 'thank you.' Before I had even let go, another guy ran up to me, kissed me on the cheek, and gave me the biggest bear hug ever. I almost had the wind knocked out of me; it was one of those hugs."

So what could this love look like for us every day? What should this demonstration of faith consist of? What do Paul's words in Galatians 5:6 mean to you?

One of the first ways we can demonstrate love with our children is to listen to them. This is harder than it seems. When they share their opinion about a topic, be it politics or their beliefs and values, rather than resist or debate, we need to listen to them and be quiet. Resisting them or defending our point of view will seldom bring about a change in their opinion anyway. How many of us have changed our mind about something because someone argued with us until we gave in?

In the book, *The Righteous Mind*, Jonathan Haidt explains that none of us take in any new information unless it comes to us in a nonthreatening manner. We need to allow our children to express what they believe. In Scripture we see that Jesus was asked 183 questions and he only answered 3 of them directly. He modeled for us how to respond. Try to empathize by saying something like, "Wow, I can see how you would feel that," with no buts.

If they are talking about politics, listen, empathize, and express in whatever way you can that you can understand how they feel. Show them love after the conversation by not withholding anything from them as a result of what was discussed. The key is to not resist, defend, give answers, or try to change what they think and feel.

When you want to ask a question, make sure it does not start with the word why. Why questions are threatening because they often contain a judgmental tone. A good question to rephrase such an inquiry is, "What led you to have that view?" or "Help me understand how you got to that place on this topic. I am really interested to know." This shows empathy and allows you the opportunity to really put yourself in their shoes, their situation, their identity or sexual orientation. Empathy and understanding build trust.

Most importantly, show them love. Ask yourself in every situation, "Will how I respond nudge them toward Jesus or push them away?" Especially if you are unaware of where your child is on their faith journey, your demonstration of faith better be better than your explanation of faith.

References:

Marin, Andrew. *Us vs. Us.* Evert & Schaupp. *I Once Was Lost.*

NIV Bible

Haidt, Jonathan. *The Righteous Mind.*

Chapter Eight

You Don't Have to Choose

When parents find out their son or daughter is gay, many times the first thing that comes to their mind is, "I am going to have to choose between my faith and my love for my son or daughter." This can be terrifying because they believe loving their child and loving God cannot coexist.

The truth is you've never had a personal connection to this topic before, at least not at this level. You've never had to search the Scriptures. You may not have known that there were six verses that talked about this. You've probably never read a book on the subject. You were just fine being uneducated on the topic. Everything changes when your child comes out.

No matter what your convictions are or what you think is or is not a sin, the love you can show them doesn't have to be limited. Jesus calls us to love one another, no matter what. This is his greatest commandment.

Like it or not, if you are a Christian, the moment your son or daughter tells you they are LGBTQ+, a theological journey begins. And you may not be aware that it is not black and white like we would like it to be or have been taught. It is gray. We don't really realize it, but we love certainty! And anything that threatens that threatens us to our very core.

Being a lover of certainty myself and loving to be in agreement with those I do life and church with, I started my own quest to know what the Bible says about homosexuality the second Noah came out. In an instant I was uncertain and conflicted because Noah did not represent who I had learned about so many years before with regard to homosexuals. He was moral. He was quiet. He loved really well. He displayed all the fruits of the Spirit. The tension from this confusion caused so much inner conflict, and I needed to get a grip on my certainty or at least be at peace with what I believed to be true about the theology surrounding homosexuality.

My journey was long and hard. It didn't help that I didn't want to be on this path, but I knew I had to be for the sake of my mental and spiritual health. Over the course of several years, God took me down roads I didn't want to travel and to places I was incredibly uncomfortable.

I am tempted to lead you through my specific journey, but doing so wouldn't be helpful. Your experience and what you learn will be unlike any other's. It is just between you and God. What God has for one person, he doesn't necessarily have for another (even if you are married).

So I will share only a general itinerary of the journey. Be open to God tweaking it to show you what he has for you to learn.

Read a book or two. Find one from someone in the progressive camp and one from a more traditional or conservative point of view. Pray for God to give you clarity as you read. Ask him to speak to you about what he wants you to know and learn.

Speak with someone you respect from both camps, whether they are straight, LGBTQ+, or parents. Do not get into a debate. This is rarely helpful.

Get to know LGBTQ+ people through reading about them or spending time with them personally. Ask them about their stories and their journeys in order to better understand how they arrived at their theological position. Stories are powerful tools for us to learn from in times like these. Do your best to listen at least 80% of the time without judgment or suspicion. Be aware of your thoughts and feelings. They can inhibit discussion and make LGBTQ+ people feel wary of or unsafe around you.

Consider connecting with a parent support group. Hearing other stories of interactions between children and their parents can be very helpful. Learning from one another can fast track your journey.

Attend a conference that speaks to issues facing LGBTQ+ individuals, and continue your dialogue with God along the way. You will experience either dissonance or peace with each new thing you learn.

Read about the nature of God. Get to know him and Jesus on a deeper level personally. Try to find out everything you can about his character and the way he loves.

Remain openhanded in case God wants to shatter some of your paradigms, like he often has with mine. Experiencing tension does not always mean something is not of God. When something is challenged you have believed all of your life, remain open to what he is trying to show you and allow him time to change or confirm what you believe.

Whether or not you believe acting on being LGBTQ+ is a sin, the truth is you are not the one choosing sin. This is between them and God. You are called to love anyway. If they are believers, the Holy Spirit will convict them of sin. This truth was so freeing to me, and I clung to it in those early days.

The key to all of this is to talk to God about what you are learning and experiencing. Your relationship with him is the most critical aspect of this process. It will be very tempting to base what you believe on what others think. This topic creates hostility and stirs strong defenses of long-held beliefs. People have definite opinions, and they want you to believe what they do. I have never seen a stronger desire for agreement from both sides on any other belief within our faith.

It's okay to be on a journey. It's okay to be confused. And it's okay not to have certainty or to know black from white. You will stay here for a while, and some of you will stay here forever. But it's important to remember that God is on this journey with you and has a purpose for you. Figuring out his purpose is the ultimate destination.

Chapter Nine

Keep It Safe

When Noah first told me he was gay, I began to test the waters with my closest, safest friends. I needed support and encouragement and couldn't bear the secret alone any longer. I did not expect the responses I received. I was not prepared for this, and at times it still breaks my heart. I was totally shocked at how some of my friends responded to the news when I finally thought it safe to tell them. The majority of my friends were kind, but some made sure I knew where they stood theologically on the topic. I was so amazed at how many times the word "sin" was brought up in early conversations. "Well, I need to let you know that I think it is a sin" and "love the sinner hate the sin" were common responses. It was like sharing with a friend that you are going through a horrible divorce and hearing them respond, "Well, I have to let you know that I think that is a sin." It was so out of place. I was so hurt.

Your friendships will change. You may not get the support you need. You may even lose friends because your son or daughter is gay or transgender.

What I discovered is that homosexuality is a topic that breeds hostility. It might even be the most controversial topic that exists within Christianity. The responses of your friends can make you doubt respected relationships and question the unconditional love you thought you knew in those friendships.

As difficult as this realization is, you are going to have to develop a thick skin and set aside peoples' responses. Someone once said you need a hard back and a soft front. There are safe people and unsafe people. Some are safe in every category except this one. I distanced myself from several close friends after Noah came out because I chose to love my child and not interfere with God's activity in his life.

It is important to assess your friendships to determine who to allow into your inner circle. You may have to decide some can be your casual friends, but not allow them to be who you turn to when you need a shoulder to lean on or someone to talk to. You need tremendous support as a parent of an LGBTQ+ child. You are suffering as well, and the presence of unsafe individuals will make the journey more difficult.

Questions like, "Who is it safe to tell and who is not?" and "Should we tell our extended family?" continually plague the mind of a closeted mom or dad. Yes, I said closeted, because many times when a gay son or daughter comes out of the closet, the parents go in.

Our first Christmas with the extended family after Noah came out, I was not prepared for the conversation that happened. We were sitting in my sister-in-law's living room when the show *Modern Family* came on TV. My usually sweet, passive mother-in-law proclaimed she didn't like the show because it was about gays and that they made her very uncomfortable. "It is just not natural," she said, as I sat there listening to her while Noah sat right beside me. I could feel my heart beating fast, my nerves shaking, and emotions overtaking my body. I was so uncomfortable because I was hearing every word through my son's ears.

Trying to redirect the conversation, I mentioned what it must have felt like, back in the day, when white people were uncomfortable with black people. She responded, "It is hardly the same. Do you really think being gay is the same thing as being black or white? Being gay is wrong. The Bible is against gays. I can show you the verses if you would like. Do you want me to show you the verses?"

To say that it was extremely unusual for my people-pleasing mother-in-law to speak this way would be an understatement. I had always known her to be so kind and loving toward any group of people. My stomach turned and my broken heart was beating rapidly as I spoke out, hoping to show my son I was there for him. "I disagree. I know there are verses, but I think they can be taken in different ways and that God is not against gays."

My mother-in-law persisted. "Debbie, you don't think it is wrong to be gay?" My 14-year-old nephew then chimed in. "I am very uncomfortable with this conversation." He too had never seen this side of his grandmother. My sister-in-law, who had not been in the room, heard what her son said, entered, and asked what in the world we were talking about. My niece chimed in, "Granny hates gays!" My sister-in-law, very surprised, asked, "What do you mean?"

I realized at this point that I needed to redirect the conversation away from the subject at hand. I was keenly aware that Noah was sitting in the corner, silent as the dead, thinking who knows what about his grandmother as well as himself. I spoke up. "One of my closest friends is gay, and she would tell you that she didn't choose this, she doesn't want it, and that she has prayed for God to take it away. I don't know of one gay person who would choose this." My sister-in-law agreed and said her experience had told her the same. At that moment I felt like my mother-in-law went for my jugular without even knowing it when she said, "Well, I think it is a choice. In fact, I think it is a result of bad influences and bad parenting that a son or daughter turns out gay." I thought I would throw up. I couldn't believe my son was hearing all this. I ached for him and wanted to get him away from this environment, but I felt helpless to do so because I knew we couldn't tell anyone why we had to leave.

When we finally left and we were in the car alone, I leaned over to my son and whispered in his ear, "You know, Noah, what Granny said to you was not okay, and I am so sorry you had to hear that." He immediately replied, "It's okay, mom."

I said, "No, it is not okay. Granny doesn't know about this subject and was raised to believe those things that are just not true." He replied, "It really doesn't bother me."

How could it not bother him? It bothered me. It tore me apart. I couldn't stop replaying the conversation in my head. It was so painful to hear someone refer to my son that way. I wanted to go home, but home was six hours away. I wanted never to talk to my mother-in-law again. I wanted to be sure Al heard what his mom had said about our son.

It bothered me so much that later that night I said to Noah, "How can you compartmentalize what happened with Granny? It is hurting me so much, and I really don't understand how it is not affecting you. Help me understand."

He replied, "Mom, I am really sorry this is hurting you, but this is the first time you have experienced this kind of conversation. This is my thirty thousandth time, and that is just with friends and family. It really just doesn't bother me anymore. I have learned to deal with it."

It stabbed me like a knife. No wonder my son had become so guarded. No wonder he had felt so rejected. No wonder he didn't feel safe to share and felt so ashamed. He knew others saw him as disgusting, so he didn't want anyone to know. I cannot even imagine having to live my life constantly waiting for the moment someone would reveal how they really felt about me. Those unintentional micro-aggressions would wear on anyone after a while.

I knew something had to be done to educate my family, friends, and community about who gay people really are. I felt we had wronged them and misjudged them. This became my personal mission.

In doing so, I could not demonize people who think differently than me or those who think the same way I used to think before my eyes were opened. My mother-in-law was not being hateful intentionally. She had not been educated on this. She was raised to believe this way, just like I was. She didn't know that the grandson she adores is one of the people she was speaking about disparagingly. Even my mother-in-law has softened on her views over the past 8 years.

We have to educate those we love by leading with love, not hate.

We need safe relationships too. This is critical for our emotional well-being. The difference is, we cannot make it our goal to make our children's friends and family safe people. They will need to do that themselves. We are only responsible for ourselves and for setting boundaries with those who are not safe.

What does setting boundaries look like? The best way to think of it is to picture two concentric circles. The inner circle contains safe people you can trust, who have compassion for you and give you their presence. There are two types of friends we have in this circle: those we can commiserate with by telling them all our woes and venting about what is really hurting or bothering us and those who are our cheerleaders. These individuals encourage us and cheer us on. They speak uplifting words when we need them and build us up. We need both types of friends in our lives, but I would put these friends in my inner circle.

Some key things to know: Not everyone needs to be part of your inner circle. You may find that people who have been safe for you for a long time are no longer safe once your son or daughter comes out. I have friends I respect and adore, friends I thought would do anything for me and who accepted me fully. But when my son came out, some of that changed. I lost some friends gradually because I discovered they were no longer safe people with whom to surround myself. This is hard and heartbreaking because it is unexpected and causes disillusionment.

Who would you define as unsafe people for you? For your son or daughter? Do you need to limit time spent with those people? It doesn't mean they cannot be part of your lives. I would just move them to the outer circle (or outside the circle altogether) if they are harmful or unloving.

Once we have figured out who we need around us, we may need to assess who needs to be around our children when the family is together. Since LGBTQ+ individuals have a smaller number of safe people they can talk to or reach out to, we could do them a great service by making sure those individuals are not around when they are.

What is at stake if we don't? A lot. Our LGBTQ+ sons and daughters already have precious few safe people or situations in which they can function, and let's face it, so do we. If we are not safe for our LGBTQ+ child, we could become depressed or suicidal as we try to deal with our current situation because we have no one else to turn to.

Not only do we need to be concerned about their mental health and safety from depression and suicide from being around unsafe rejecting people. We also need to be aware of the fact that if we or other people are unsafe for our kids

The Big Reveal

and call ourselves Christians, that unsafe feeling will impact how they feel about church and God as well.

You may decide certain people are safe to talk to about this with and others are not. There are still some people we have chosen not to tell about Noah because doing so would harm him. Look at every relationship and ask this question: "Is it safe for this person to know?"

Chapter Ten

You Will Be Okay

I wrote down these phrases to remind myself again and again: "I am going to be okay." "Noah is going to be okay." "Our family is going to be okay." It may not feel like it, but you are going to be okay.

In the beginning, there were times I could hardly breathe. Every day I was learning new things about the secret life of my child, and each discovery required me to accept a new reality. You may have found out they are gay or transgender, that they have a girlfriend or boyfriend, that they don't believe in God any longer, or you may have discovered they no longer think of themselves as the son or daughter you brought into this world and to whom you gave lots of thought to the name you would give them. All these new realities can seem too painful to bear. Sometimes I still feel this way, but years later it has gotten easier.

I have found peace on this journey, and so will you. In the beginning, everything is a new piece of information learned, a trauma to process, a depression to move through. Practice taking one day at a time, and do not expect too much from yourself. Surround yourself with care and grace and loving friends you can commiserate with. If you can't find any who are safe, connect online with a parent support group. Parent Connect, Embracing the Journey, Harbor, and others are available. Cry out to God. He loves and cares about you, and he loves and cares about your child. It will not be this way forever. It just feels like that now. Remind yourself you are not alone.

When my daughter was struggling with her mental health, which to say the least has been a journey all its own, my husband and I were at a loss to know what to do with mental illness being a part of our family. We decided to go to a class the National Alliance on Mental Illness calls "Family-to-Family." In the session, we learned the stages a family goes through as they navigate the journey of coming to terms with having a child with a mental illness. This knowledge was so informative and helpful.

I have found these same stages can be applied to what parents go through when they find out their son or daughter is gay or transgender.

The Stages:
Shock/Crisis
Education
Acceptance
Advocacy

Finding out your son or daughter has lived a secret life and has done so for some time is incredibly traumatic. It can feel like a shock to your system to find out the person you love so much has a side to them you have not known before now. They have been navigating life alone, without you, and many times did not feel safe to tell you. It can be heartbreaking to recognize they didn't feel safe with you.

The shock and crisis stage was very real for me and

Al from the moment Noah told us. As I mentioned before, I instantly felt nauseous from the stress. It felt like our son had been killed in a car accident, and we hadn't had a chance to say goodbye. The grief of shattered dreams was overwhelming. I was in a daze for days. I couldn't think straight or make decisions, and I obsessed over our new reality constantly.

A few weeks after Noah's reveal, I remember talking to him on the phone and asking him when he would be home from a friend's house. I wanted to talk and get to know the part of him I had missed out on the last four years. His response to my question was difficult to hear. "Mom, I have another life, and it would take too long to catch you up on the person I am now." As it turned out, he didn't have two lives, two sides. He had one persona that was real and one that he'd manufactured, he explained. It was the fake one I had known the last four years.

But if coming to terms with their new identity was all there was to navigate, doing so might be possible with minimal crisis and trauma. But on top of that, you have to deal with your family, your friends, your church, and your relationship with God. The list can seem to go on and on. Many times this is so much to bear emotionally that parents go into shock or crisis mode. This stage can last quite a while. How long it takes to move through this stage depends on how long it takes to navigate each aspect of your new reality.

Education

The second stage involves educating yourself by reading everything you can get your hands on and learning everything there is to know about homosexuality or being transgender. You learn what your son or daughter is going through, what the Bible has to say about it, and scour for helpful details in every book, blog, podcast, and sermon you can find on the topic.

Two weeks after The Reveal I signed up for my first conference for LGBTQ+ Christians. I took so many notes in the main sessions and the breakouts. I bought all the books they offered as resources. When I got home, I started reading the books and blogs and listening to more talks on the subject. I couldn't get enough.

During the next eight years, my reading topic of choice was most often homosexuality. My bibliography is wide-ranging, from conservative to progressive.

If I attended a conference to meet some of my required continuing education hours to maintain my license as a counselor, I would make sure to sign up for any breakout related to homosexuality if one was offered.

I talked for hours to those who were a part of the LGBTQ+ community, learning from the stories of their experiences. As each one shared their perspective, I would understand more about Noah. The relationships I developed during those years were my favorite part of the education stage. Most of what I have learned about LGBTQ+ individuals has come from talking to them.

Acceptance

It can take a few years, but more than likely you will come to accept that your son or daughter is LGBTQ+. This stage is characterized by not caring as much who knows or what people think of you as a parent. You are secure in your love for your child and are learning how to love them well and how to navigate the special circumstances that come with loving someone who is LGBTQ+.

The Big Reveal

I got to this point really fast, and I am so thankful God allowed me to. I firmly believe that if I hadn't, my son would not be alive today. Noah's depression was so deep that if I had stayed in the shock/crisis phase or the education phase too long, it would have been more than he could bear.

What I found strange though is that the acceptance stage has had several phases. The first phase involved accepting who Noah is and recognizing he hasn't chosen to be gay.

The next phase involved telling more and more people, but preparing for their possible responses and feeling awful if they reacted poorly.

In the last phase of acceptance, I am now able to share with anyone that Noah is gay and (for the most part) not be concerned with what their responses will be, whether positive or negative. I am secure in who he is and who I am, and I don't let their opinion or approval (or lack thereof) ruin my day or determine my mood.

Like I said, it's good that I made it to the acceptance stage quickly. Noah has always craved acceptance. He loves pleasing people. Rejection is harder on him than the average young adult. God knew he needed his family to surround him, to let him know how much we love him no matter what, and to stand beside him. He carries so much shame for his identity that I believe it will take him years to heal. He is working on that in counseling, and my hope and prayer is that he will someday be able to come to grips with who he is and how much God loves him.

I don't take for granted that I took the fast track to the acceptance stage. I know it was a gift God didn't have to give me. Many others do not experience this, and they struggle much longer in the other phases. I am also very aware that it was not my doing that I came to a place of acceptance so quickly. If it were up to me, I would have been stuck in the first phase indefinitely. I know how to wallow in misery.

Advocacy

When you come to this stage, watch out, world! There is a reason there are groups of parents of LGBTQ+ children called "Mama Bears" and "Papa Bears." When we take on advocating for our children, we are a force to be reckoned with. I want to see injustices to the LGBTQ+ community (or to anyone marginalized, for that matter) made right.

My first experience with advocacy took place before attending a conference. I had learned that there would be a time at the event when any parent could line up, and LGBTQ+ individuals wanting a hug from a parent could come through the line and receive as many as they want. I purchased a sweatshirt with the message "Free Mom Hugs" to wear. Many of these individuals had very strained or no relationship with their parents after coming out. Some of them longed for this affection and comfort from a mother or father figure who accepted them.

I gave several hugs that day, and with each hug my anguish grew for this community and the love that is often withheld from them. My own "mama bear" tendencies came to life at that conference and have only grown since.

We want so badly to protect our children from pain, but it is so much more than that. We want to educate others, for we realize there was a time when we were unaware of these issues and what it is really like to be LGBTQ+. Now we know and want others to be enlightened as well. We want them to understand that our sons and daughters are really good people with really good hearts. We want others to know that their categories and stereotypes for people can change. We understand what it's like to be unaware because we too may have grown up believing and being taught certain things that were not true.

We want others to know our kids are not choosing this!

The Big Reveal

They are just trying to live normal lives. We know they do not want to be treated differently or seen only as gay or transgender. We know they want to be valued in society as diverse people with so many other interesting qualities.

We want others to know the pain this group is experiencing is so unnecessary. We want them to know that they are being shut out by the church and rejected by Christians who follow a God who doesn't feel that way about them. We want them to know the Jesus of the Bible, who sat at all the tables and ate with everyone. We want them to know that he loves them and that they are his children too.

But most of all, our number one goal is for everyone to learn how to love one another and eliminate the hate that divides us.

Not every parent becomes an advocate or even reaches the acceptance stage, for that matter. Many get stuck in shock/crisis, and others are not open to the education available to them. The difficulty with this is that our LGBTQ+ children will not feel the love every child deserves from their parents because some remain stuck in these stages. If you are one of those parents, I urge you to seek some therapy to learn how to grieve well. Your mental health and that of your child could depend on it. I believe working through the stages is critical to your and your child's well-being.

References:

National Alliance on Mental Illness, Family-to-Family Course

Conclusion: The Ultimate Reveal

My husband and I really thought the big reveal of our lives was when our son came out to us in 2014. I didn't think anything could top it or shake us more.

But it's important to remember this: **God has entrusted you with this story.** Oh, how those words comforted me when Aaron told me that just a week after Noah came out. It changed my perspective immediately and gave me a new purpose.

Although you may not realize it, God has many things for you in this journey. He has things to show you, to teach you, and he wants to work through you. This is your child's journey and yours as well.

Although not a story you would have chosen, God has meaning and purpose that will result from it. He chose you to be your child's mother or father. We have been selected to carry this story with our child, so they don't have to carry it alone. It may not feel like you will ever see the purpose of this journey, but one day you might be surprised to find yourself thankful for the story and the perspective change it has brought to your life as a result.

For me, being Noah's mother has opened my eyes to a hurting group of people I never would have seen otherwise. I see everything so differently now, and my compassion overflows for each and every LGBTQ+ person I meet. It might be really hard to even imagine that God could use this story to change others, but it will, and the first life it will change is your own.

After Noah revealed to us that he is gay, I didn't realize that the ultimate reveal would be something far greater: my heart would explode with love for so many different people.

The ultimate reveal ended up being the discovery of the condition of my heart toward a specific group of people. I saw condemnation there, disgust, and misjudgment of the LGBTQ+ community, which is often more accepting, loving, less condemning, and godly than I could have ever imagined—certainly more than me.

I couldn't have been more wrong about this group as a whole. In the past eight years, I have encountered so many people very similar to Noah, people who are kind, accepting, forgiving, gracious, moral, and—most of the time—not pushing an agenda. What I realized is that the image I had in my head of a gay person does, in fact, exist, but my caricature was not true of the majority, and believing that was my fault.

When people are rejected, they seek acceptance from whoever will give it to them. They run away from rejecting Christians to a community in which they can belong.

Many LGBTQ+ people I have met love Jesus and experience freedom in him. I have encountered many who want to learn more about Jesus and how to share his love with others. I'll never forget going to a conference for this demographic soon after Noah came out and being overwhelmed by the number of people singing praises to Jesus in complete freedom and expressing genuine love for him. I had never experienced this with straight Christians! Before this conference my perception of LGBTQ+ Christians was that they would be experiencing the consequences of their sin and hiding from God. In short, the opposite of free.

What I experienced that day forever transformed me and shattered my paradigm.

I once thought the ultimate reveal of my life was when my son told me about himself and his sexual orientation. I now realize the true ultimate reveal was what God has shown *me* through this journey about who I was and what I have yet to become. I had become judgmental and unloving toward others. I never thought Jesus could show me what true love is through the revelation of someone's sexual orientation, but he did. The love I have now for others—whether they are gay, straight, transgender, mentally ill, tatted up, or pierced from head to toe—is overwhelming. I would not be who I am without this custom-made story God has entrusted to my family. And I am so grateful. He answered a prayer I prayed two years before Noah's reveal with the words from Hillsong's "Hosanna":

"Heal my heart and make it clean, Open up my eyes to the things unseen, Show me how to love like you have loved me. Break my heart for what breaks yours."

He continues to do all of that, and I am so thankful for what he has shown me—The Ultimate Reveal of God's love for all people.

References

Marin, A. *Us vs. Us*

Schaupp, D. & Everts, D. *I Once Was Lost*

Sexual Orientation and Estimates of Adult Substance Use and Mental Health: Results from the 2015 National Survey on Drug Use and Health

Medley, G., Lipari, R. N., Bose, J., Cribb, D. S., Kroutil, L. A., & McHenry, G. (2016, October).

Wanta, et al. "Mental Health Diagnoses Among Transgender Patients in the Clinical Setting: An All-Payer Electronic Health Record Study." Transgender Health, 4.1, 2019.

Price-Feeney et al. "Understanding the Mental Health of Transgender and Nonbinary." Journal of Adolescent Health | Volume 66, ISSUE 6, P684-690, January, 2020.

Park, H. and Mykhyalyshyn, L. "L.G.B.T. People Are More Likely to Be Targets of Hate Crimes Than Any Other Minority Group." June, 2016.

Human Rights Campaign Foundation and researchers at the University of Connecticut. "Growing Up LGBT in America." 2017

Kosciw, J. G. et al, "The 2019 National School Climate Survey: The experiences of lesbian, gay, bisexual, transgender, and queer youth in our nation's schools." New York: GLSEN. 2020

Kann, L. et al. "Youth risk behavior surveillance." MMWR Surveill Summ. 2018; 67: 1–114.

Haidt, J. *The Righteous Mind*

National Alliance on Mental Illness – Family-to-Family

Hillsong. "Hosanna." Hillsong United.

NIV: THE HOLY BIBLE, NEW INTERNATIONAL VERSION®, NIV® Copyright© 1973, 1978, 1984, 2011 by Biblica, Inc.™ Used by permission. All rights reserved worldwide.

About the Author

Debbie Causey is a licensed counselor, ordained pastor at a megachurch, and a mother who has been on a journey to discover what God has to say about the topic of homosexuality and gender identity issues and the LGBTQ+ community for the past decade. She leads a ministry for parents of LGBTQ+ children who are desperate to learn how to love their children well and discover God's purposes for them on this journey. She has spoken at several conferences about parenting LGBTQ+ children well and is passionate about seeing LGBTQ+ individuals and their families reconciled to each other and their faith.